THE PROSPERI

Restoring Your Inner Peace After Abuse
The Individual Book

KNOW YOUR WORTH **FATHER GOD**
PRICELESS RIGHTS **PROVIDER**
LOVE **HEALER**
KINDNESS **PROTECTOR**
FORGIVENESS **ALL MIGHTY**
GREAT GRACES **WAY MAKER**

Prosperity

After your storm will come your blessing.

This guide is written from one survivor to the next.

Michelle Carter-Douglass

THE PROSPERITY PROJECT PRESENTS:
Restoring Your Inner Peace After Abuse
The Individual Book
© 2018 Michelle Carter-Douglass

Tres Luces Publishing dba WCD Professional Services
Tres Luces Publishing is committed to finding a focus on solutions to epidemics that plague our communities. Through art and literature, we strive to bring awareness and alternative resolutions for the stressors of our world today.

Minister Michelle Carter-Douglass is available for motivational speaking and all speaking engagements. Please refer to your interest in booking her appearance by calling (330)881-3434.

Book Formatting and set-up designed by Michelle Carter-Douglass of WCD Professional Services LLC

*All scripture references are taken from The King James Version of The Holy Bible and unedited.

Almighty God

Thank You, Oh, Heavenly Father. You remain with me through all of the rain and storms. You, Oh God, have sheltered and comforted me. With Your Holy Finger Tips pressed upon my face, ever so gently, You, wipe the tears.

Without the darkness from the world and within, I could never embrace the Light from Heaven's expanse. You have protected me from being consumed by all of the windstorms and hail.

You have opened and closed many doors throughout my journey. The idle talk, and devilish gossip, from others, have both seasoned and hurt my heart.

I will share all of my storms, thoughts, and glory through written chapters of my works. I dedicate everything I do to serving You. In my happiness, I bestow gratitude to my Heavenly Father on High. I thank You for the spiritual growth, and I am forever in Servitude to You, my Almighty God.

The Lord's Prayer Matthew 6:9-13 (KJV)

Our Father, who art in heaven,

hallowed be thy Name,

thy kingdom come,

thy will be done,

on earth as it is in heaven.

Give us this day our daily bread.

And forgive us our trespasses,

as we forgive those

who trespass against us.

And lead us not into temptation,

but deliver us from evil.

For thine is the kingdom,

and the power, and the glory,

for ever and ever.

Amen

Table of Contents

Gratitude

Upon these pages, I send praise to Almighty God, for You have given us Your undivided attention, love, and support. I finally understand that I am blessed with the spirit of kindness and giving back, as well as loving my enemies, family, readers, and friends. Heavenly Father, I love You with all of my heart and soul!

Thank You!

I send my love and appreciation to my children, Patrick M. Douglass, Arlessa R. Douglass, Brialan M. Douglass (Ricky Lisa N Bry YouTube Channel), and Kailah M. Douglass, my mother, Patricia Ann Carter, my family friends, and those that helped me raise my children: Warnetta Millhouse, Irma Casey, John Wilson, Darlene Culver, Jerome Wilson, Nicole Carter, Jennifer Wilson, Jaylynn Wilson, Jevin Wilson, DeAna Culver, Danielle Culver, Patrice Henderson, Jake Larkin, Cortland Casey, Cortland Casey Sr., Valarie Casey, Anissa Casey, Amina

Mason, Bobby Croom, Jeramiah Croom, Patrick Manigat, The Manigat Family, Desmond Mohammad, The Mohammad Family, Alanne Rouse, The Rouse Family, TJ, Marcus, Bertha Smith, The Smith Family, Anita Gomez, Angelo Gomez, The Gomez Family, Julia Lugo, Carmen Rodriguez, The Rodriguez Family, The Lugo Family, Stacie Erin Hunter, The Hunter Family, The Cochran Family, Mary Arleta Cochran, The Ferguson Family, Shannon Cassedy-Gray, Aida Reynolds, Patrick Reynolds, Andre Reynolds, Angelisa, James Reynolds, Mem, Cataleya, Camden, Reverand Travis Evans of The Encouragement Circle, Mrs. Gennette Thompson Evans, Mr. & Mrs. Herman & Donna Harcum.

Hello,

It doesn't matter what you have gone through in your life; you matter. The hurt that other people place upon you does not define you. Your trials and tribulations will strengthen you. Through this book, you will learn your strengths and possess the skills to heal from your experiences. Ultimately, you will gain resilience and retain your happiness.

Healing from abuse, the victim has to take control of their strength and power.

Some of us have heard words that left us to question our worth. Now, it is time to listen to the voice of God.

Psalm 139:14, "I will praise thee; for I am fearfully and wonderfully made: marvelous are thy works; and that my soul knoweth right well."

We can be bitter about our troubles. We can refuse to forgive those who taunt us. You and I can hurt everyone who has harmed us. However, that won't heal the emotional wounds or remove the emotional scars. Vengeance can never take back the harm. Hurting others will only hinder us from moving forward in life.

Time is too short to remain imprisoned by pain. You have too much to offer the world, and there are people who need you. I hope this book and study guide will help you or a person you know to heal.

Know your worth and shine brightly during your storms and accomplishments. Never allow anyone nor anything to dim your marvelous lights.

Sincerely,

Michelle Carter-Douglass

1

You Are Priceless
(Knowing your worth)

Right now, stop all the negative thinking. Whatever is mentally overwhelming you, we are giving it to The Lord. The time is here to re-develop your relationship with you. Yes, you deserve a healthy and strong relationship with yourself.

Through this book and study guide, we will work through what's preventing you from having a great relationship with yourself. Next, stop allowing others to discount your worth. It is all right to set boundaries and tell people no.

Also, you and I will address what has hindered your perception of yourself and your value. Possibly, unaddressed emotions of our experiences hinder our self-perceptions. At times, we dwell in depression because we are afraid, to be honest about our real emotions. We want to make ourselves and others think we have let go of the pain while it lies dormant within our soul.

Acknowledging Our Hardships & Pain

By acknowledging our heartaches and pain, survivors must allow themselves to recall traumatic experiences that affected them. I experienced bullying throughout my entire life. These traumatic experiences affected my esteem, decision-making, and anxiety issues. As an adolescent and adult woman, I allowed other people to determine my value.

I looked for praise in all the wrong places. I began a promiscuous behavior, and I ultimately lost the value within myself. I thought I was worthless. I no longer expected much in life, nor of myself. In not knowing my worth, I allowed others to negotiate my value.

The question is, what traumatic experience created the devaluation of yourself? *Take a moment to reflect.*

No person can determine your worth because only you have walked in your shoes. Subconsciously and internally, we know that no person should deem our value. When we allow someone to determine our worth, we feel robbed. We must acknowledge our trauma, then address the trauma, and ultimately reach the healing core to reconnect with our worth.

For many years, I refused to acknowledge my heartaches and pain. My thought, in ignoring my traumatic experiences, they would dissipate. **WRONG!**

For me to heal, I had to acknowledge and address the wounds.

Example: You're walking to a nearby store to purchase a gallon of milk. Suddenly you step on a nail! The question is, do you remove the object and continue walking to the store? Or, do you acknowledge the wound and address seeking medical attention?

In traumatic experiences, we are prone to recognize imminent dangers or problems. However, we refuse to acknowledge or address them.

Explanation: We think by removing the nail and continuing walking, the wound will heal on its own.

Some people may not have religion-based healing. A few individuals believe in a divine being that relates to the atmosphere. Some people may even steer away from conventional religions or belief systems. I have wrestled with God in my faith. While writing this book, I explored all considerations of the delicacy of addressing the healing core without forcing religious beliefs on the survivor. Although I speak of God and my faith, it is not the core of the healing system. This book focuses on the strength-based perspective and addresses the need for acknowledgment of real and honest emotions. My belief is that we cannot heal from the trauma if we refuse to acknowledge the hurt and pain.

For my healing journey, I look to God and The Holy Bible. The Bible consists of imperfect people who faced many obstacles and persecutions. Often times we are able to see more clearly by examples of others.

2 Timothy 3:16, "All scripture is given by inspiration of God and is profitable for doctrine, for reproof, for correction, for instruction in righteousness:" I believe in a higher being and I believe in The Holy Bible.

I also know there is a lower entity. That lower entity tries its hardest to draw out our energy. To receive inspiration and instruction, I read The Bible.

Sometimes, we feel at war in the community, at our jobs, and behind closed doors. After dealing with health issues, financial issues, relationship issues, spiritual warfare, and mental issues, having no strength to embrace our worth. Soon, we become distanced from who we are. That is how the enemy attacks. He throws everything at us at once. When we forget who we are, we forget whose we are. We are separated from our purpose and unable to see our worth.

Soon those "*emotional quicksand*" questions creep in: "Why am I here?" "Am I a good parent?" "Have I done all that I can in life?" "Am I being punished?"

These questions drive us deeper into emotional and mental quicksand. What is *emotional and mental quicksand*?

To understand this mental and emotional state of mind, we must define quicksand first.

Mental and Emotional Quicksand

Quicksand, defined by Merriam Webster Dictionary, is "a bottomless and movable bulk of sand. This substance, when mixed with water into which heavy objects readily sink. The formed substance (quicksand) thus entraps and frustrates whatever it consumes."

Take a mental note of these vocabulary words: *Bottomless, movable, bulk, mixed, water, sink, entrap and frustrate.*

These words we will discuss more closely later in the chapter.

Currently, we will define and differentiate what our emotions are and what our mental state is.

The question is, Are emotions the same thing as our mental state of mind? The answer is no. Emotions and our mental state of mind are two separate matters. However, both are a direct cause in the effect of one another.

Please take note of the two words "*emotions*" and "*mental.*" We will discuss these words later as well.

Reader, close your eyes and listen to your inner strength who has a voice. Embrace the power to choose happiness and safety. You have strength on this healing journey.

With your eyes closed, envision:

The power to choose your destiny.

You can choose your company.

The strength to choose who you love.

You can choose what you will and won't accept from people in your life. You do not deserve unhappiness or fear. *Open your eyes now and envision freedom from pain and sorrow.*

Now, let's explore *quicksand* more closely. *Quicksand* "is a bottomless and movable bulk of sand. This substance as mixed with water into which heavy objects readily sink. The formed substance (*quicksand*) thus entraps and hinders whatever it consumes." (Merriam-Webster Dictionary)

When you think or hear of something bottomless, you contemplate that this is without end. Grief and depression are overwhelming to many people.

Reflecting earlier in the chapter about issues that we may face in everyday life, such as health issues, family issues, financial issues, and community issues, these epidemics and struggles can be part of the quicksand bottomless thinking. Meaning you might feel as though the problems will never go away. These issues will only become worse. These issues are like sand being mixed with the water of pessimistic thoughts. You have formed "*quicksand.*"

Now, you and I will explore the **bulk** thinking of quicksand. We may think our problems are too immense to overcome. You, or I may see our problems as weights placed upon our bodies that won't move. Here we begin to sink in the very quicksand formed within our minds. Here we dwell in a darkness that we believe there is no light. *Quicksand* entraps you to frustrate your movement and growth. The quicksand wants your energy! You do not need a substance to thrive; the substance needs you to survive. The enemy wants you entrapped to prevent you from doing The Will of God. The adversary wants you annoyed and upset. Why you may ask???,???,???

Because he does not want you to achieve your purpose and blessing. The adversary doesn't want you to grow nor change.

Now that we have defined what quicksand is and how it affects our minds, goals, and happiness, let's evaluate what *emotions* and the *mental* are and how they differ. "*Emotions* are a natural instinctive state of mind. Meaning that *emotions* are a natural innate state of perception. *Emotions* come naturally to a person, and it is a strong feeling directed toward someone or something, deriving from an individual's circumstance, mood, and or relationship with others. *Emotions* are typically accompanied by the physiological and behavioral changes in the body." (Merriam-Webster Dictionary)

Happiness, sadness, anger, calmness, pleasure, and fear are natural emotions that everyone experience in their lives. Instinctive feelings, or real emotions will never deprive us of our worth, nor are they wrong. Our Heavenly Father experiences happiness and sadness.

Note scriptures, *Jeremiah 32:40-42, John 15:10-12, Deuteronomy 9:7-20, and Job 4:8-10*.

The denial of our emotions brings about the negative outcome from the perceptions of our real emotions that can hinder us.

Now to characterize "the mental". Mental defined by Merriam-Webster Dictionary is "relating to the mind; specifically of or relating to the total emotional and intellectual response to the individual's external reality." Our emotions are natural feelings, and the mental is the outcome and or the response of what we feel.

In *Deuteronomy 9:7-20*, Moses is angry at what the Israelites did while he was on the mountain speaking with our Heavenly Father. Noted in these scriptures is the anger from our Lord as well. Moses being upset was not entirely a sin. It was what he did while he was angry that angered our God. In *Job 4:8-10*, Job speaks about the anger and evil of others and declares the outcome from the anger of God.

God also has love and happiness in His heart and soul, *Jeremiah 32:40-42 NIV*, "I will rejoice in doing them good and will assuredly plant them in this land with all my heart and soul."

Another example of God wanting the best for us is *John 15:10-12 NIV*, " If you keep my commands, you will remain in my love, just as I have kept my Father's commands and remain in his love. [11] I have told you this so that my joy may be in you and that your joy may be complete. [12] My command is this: Love each other as I have loved you."

Our abusers lack love in their hearts. The powerless quicksand formed by oppression and pain has no power to love anyone or anything. Take another step-in freedom, forgiveness, and love by removing the powerless quicksand from your minds.

As you alleviate yourself from those toxic memories and thoughts, your mind will heal. A way the enemy deprives God's children of their blessings, is to attack our minds. The adversary uses our health, financial issues, relationship issues, and mental issues against us. He drains us to where our minds cannot be spiritually fed.

Reflect & think: [a] When we are not emotionally right, we are not emotionally with Christ.

[b] When we are not mentally alright, we can't be used by Christ. [c] When we are separated from Almighty God, our Lord and Savior Jesus Christ, we forget about our purpose. Through deprivation of worth in our spirits, we doubt our purpose in our lives. In time, we harbor resentment toward those who hurt us.

Privation of Christ and our purpose drives us deeper into emotional and mental quicksand.

Through these healing Journies, there are two factors you must acknowledge.

Factor #1, You have the ability to forgive.

Factor #2, You have the ability to harbor resentment and pain.

The pain we endured was definitely wrong and not deserved. However, as wrong as those injustices were, they were not uncommon. _Bad things happen to good people from bad people._

Reflect & think: How many of us have been called names? How many of us were hit?

We all were talked about, discriminated against, lied to, lied on, or looked down on.

Yet, how many of us have been able to forgive and forget.

It is hard, but as long as we are stuck in that emotional and mental quicksand, we are still their victim. Remember, quicksand is a movable bulk. Meaning it is capable of being moved.

Ready to take the next steps in your journey?

   ✓ Give those bags of sand to Almighty God.

✓ Call on our Lord and Savior, Jesus Christ.

✓ Watch and feel your burdens lift.

Earlier discussed in the chapter, *quicksand only forms when water adds to its substance.* Instead of wasting water on your troubles, take that same water, and wash free of them. **Romans 8:6**, "[6] For to be carnally minded is death, but to be spiritually minded is life and peace." Unforgiveness, vengeance, and loathing are carnal-minded deaths. You cannot live in happiness; if we are dead in our minds.

Stimulative thought perspective, you have the power to choose greatness daily. You and I can forgive, persevere, become wiser, show kindness and allow our spiritual light to grow. As long as we're stuck in emotional and mental quicksand, we are victims. We give our power to the enemy for possession over us. The enemy attacks through trials and tribulations because he doesn't want you to achieve your purpose and know your worth.

The reason people face trials isn't the idea they are bad people; it is because they are God's people. You are the children of The Highest God and have favor in His eyes. Your light is shining so bright in the gut of darkness. You have a gift so powerful the adversary is afraid.

Know your worth, heal from what has hurt you, and make the adversary afraid. The people who hurt you, let them go and love them from afar. Take these next steps in your healing journey to aid in the awareness of who you are.

Once you re-establish who you are, you will know whose you are. **2 Corinthians 3:16-18 NIV**, "But whenever anyone turns to the Lord, the veil is taken away. [17] Now the Lord is the Spirit, and where the Spirit of the Lord is, there is freedom. [18] And we all, who with unveiled faces contemplate the Lord's glory, are being transformed into his image with ever-increasing glory, which comes from the Lord, who is the Spirit."

Healing Journey Steps:

✓ Discover your likes and dislikes. (Identifying your likes and dislikes helps in establishing your hobbies.)

✓ Set boundaries.

✓ Build and connect with your hobbies.

Once the foundation establishes, your purpose becomes more defined. Through the definition of purpose, you discover your worth. When you understand and embrace your worth, everything falls into place. Your relationship with The Lord strengthens. Your relationship with you strengthens. You will not only enjoy your hobbies, but you will also find them fulfilling. You will begin to set sound boundaries that will bring you absolute peace of mind.

1

You Are Priceless
(Knowing your worth)

Study Guide

Chapter Scriptures

Jeremiah 32:40-42

John 15:10-12

Deuteronomy 9:7-20

Job 4:8-10

2 Timothy 3:16

Romans 8:6

2 Corinthians 3:16-18

Chapter Vocabulary Words

quicksand	Mixed	Frustrate
Bottomless	Water	Emotions
Movable	Sink	Mental
Bulk	Entrap	Carnal

Quicksand:

_____

_____

_____

_____

Bottomless:

_____

_____

_____

_____

Movable:

_____

_____

_____

_____

Bulk:

_____

_____

_____

_____

Mixed:

_____

_____

_____

_____

Water:

_____

_____
_____
_____

Sink:

_____
_____
_____
_____

Entrap:

_____
_____
_____
_____

Frustrate:

_____
_____
_____
_____

Emotions:

_____
_____
_____
_____

Mental:

_____
_____
_____
_____
_____

Carnal:

_____
_____
_____
_____

QUESTIONS & ANSWER SECTION

1. Do you have a purpose? _____ Why or why not?

_____
_____
_____
_____
_____
_____

2. Do you have a worth? _____ Why or why not?

_____
_____

_____

_____

_____

_____

_____

3. Can someone walk up to you and place a price tag on you? _____ Please explain your answer.

_____

_____

_____

_____

_____

4. [a]Think about how you would feel if a random person or persons walked up to you and began placing a price tag on you. [b] Take, the time to describe below how this behavior would be acceptable or unacceptable to you.

_____

_____

_____

_____

_____

_____

_____

_____

_____

_____

5. What Book and Chapter are these scriptures found in? _____

   [13] For thou hast possessed my reins: thou hast covered me in my mother's womb. [14] I will praise thee; for I am fearfully and wonderfully made: marvellous are thy works; and that my soul knoweth right well.

6. What is emotional and mental quicksand?

   _____
   _____
   _____
   _____
   _____

7. What are some things that can hinder our relationship with self?

   a. _____
   b. _____
   c. _____
   d. _____
   e. _____

8. Who tries to dim our lights by using tactics, lies, and trickery? _____ Please explain your answer.

   _____
   _____

_____
_____
_____
_____
_____
_____
_____

9. What must we do to achieve happiness and peace in our lives?

     a. _____

     b. _____

     c. _____

     d. _____

     e. _____

TRUE OR FALSE

1. _____ All scripture is given by inspiration of God, and is profitable for doctrine, reproof and instruction.

2. _____ The enemy does not use tricks to mislead us.

3. _____ When we are deprived, of our, purpose we doubt our worth.

4. _____ Quicksand is a bottomless and movable bulk of sand mixed with water into which heavy objects readily sink.

5. _____ Emotions and the mental are the same.

6. _____ We have no power over our daily choices.

7. _____ Our God is bigger than our trials and tribulations.

2

Defining and Working Through Real Emotions

Today when I awoke, I peered through my window to embrace the morning horizon. I enjoyed the view of the sky, the birds flying so high, and the wind's movement on the branches of the trees. I enjoyed the "*real*" vibrations and life in the world. What I saw was *real* and tangible.

Real is defined by Oxford Languages Online Dictionary as "actually existing as a thing or occurs, not imagined or supposed."

We all have heard and dealt with emotions such as *anger, contentment, sadness, happiness, fear, courage, pleasure, and uncomfort*. Emotions are real, come naturally, and are seen by others. Emotions, like the wind, can be felt by others. But at times, our emotions are clouded by our perceptions. We are unable to distinguish between *reality* and *fiction*.

For example, how do we know the wind produces the movements of the tree's branches?

The movement of the branches is our perception through senses and teachings. Individual *perception* is "the ability to see, hear, or become aware of something through the senses." (Oxford Languages Online Dictionary.)

The *senses* " are a faculty by which the body perceives an external stimulus; one of the faculties of sight, smell, hearing, taste, and touch." (Oxford Languages Online Dictionary.)

Life's struggles can hinder our ability to decipher between real emotions and counterfeit emotions.

Pondering Questions,

? What are real and counterfeit emotions exactly?

? How do they affect our ability to know our worth?

? How do real emotions differ from counterfeit emotions?

? In our own lives and situations, how did we replace our *real emotions* with *counterfeit emotions*?

In the previous chapter, we discussed acknowledging our hardships and pain, hindering our perceptions of self, bitterness, lack of forgiveness, and defined emotional quicksand. The enemy can use denial of our true feelings and or emotions that lead to feelings of *hopelessness, depression, and displaced anger.* The goal of this chapter will be detecting our counterfeit emotions, identifying our real emotions, and working through them.

The Overall Objective of This Chapter:

✓ Define real and counterfeit emotions.

✓ Address the lack of honesty with our real emotions. (The inability to acknowledge your real feelings and emotions can distance your personal relationship with yourself and others.)

✓ Acknowledge and recognize how we might have used counterfeit emotions to mask our real emotions.

As I affirmed earlier, if you cannot be "real" with yourself, you will not be honest or "true" with anyone. Your instinctive emotions exist, *Behind Closed Doors*. You can choose not to acknowledge your true feelings or emotions; however, you can't hide your true feelings.

Identifying Scenario 1

Imagine you are at a neighboring park on a warm autumn's day and people are laughing, talking, and playing outdoor games.

There is a disabled man who has difficulty standing and has to use a cane. He smiles ever so brightly as he enjoys watching a group of young adults playing basketball. The disabled man's name is Tom. Tom was diagnosed at the age of two with spinal bifida. The doctors indicated he would never walk or run; his mother knew otherwise. Tom has always desired to participate in outdoor activities, especially basketball. Tom is cheering random players on and enjoying the game as two adolescent males rudely brush past him, and the second male says in a nasty quiet undertone voice to Tom, "Hey cripple, stay out the way!"

True Thoughts

1) What was your first feeling and emotion?

   a. Were you angry, shocked, saddened, amused, etc.?

Real emotions are feelings that are instinctive and come naturally. If someone resorts to calling you names, you might feel sad, angry, or hurt. If someone resorts to physical violence you may feel anger or fear. *Counterfeit or masked emotions* are untrue feelings that you display in front of others or to the other-self in order to receive an expected response. Yes, very long but very true.

For example, in the identifying scenario above, a person who has witnessed this heinous action might feel anger or sadness as the first instinctive feeling. For a moment let you and I remove our "Good Samaritan" shoes and place the shoes of a bully on our feet. This individual is more like the tyrants, and perhaps this individual witnessing the act has the instinctive feeling of contentment or happiness

41

as the real emotion. Thus, because he or she is around others, they choose to mask their feelings with anger as a counterfeit emotion. So, he or she will show anger because this is the expected emotion someone should feel.

Growing up, I saw and endured so much in my life. I became aware of people who wore masks. In front of others, they appeared to be one way, and behind those closed doors, they were another. I vowed at a young age never to be like them. Sometimes, I think this was both a blessing and a hindrance. I chose not to hide from anyone; when I made mistakes, people knew. Yes, I vowed never to be like the "pretenders," however, to adapt to situations, I learned to suppress my expressions of my *real emotions*.

Over time, I am learning to suppress my show of fear and anger. Throughout my life, I have experienced anger, contentment, sadness, happiness, fear, courage, pleasure, and uncomfort.

Identifying Scenario 2 (a)

Visualize, you are a student in high school who is a bit of a loner. You love to read, and your sense of fun is visiting the local library and church. Your name, is Leigh. You are made fun of because you are not conforming to the majority's definition of entertainment. Because of your peers and their mockery, you begin to doubt your purpose and judgment. You even start to ponder what it would be like to be popular.

Be asked to school dances and dates. Suddenly you receive a note in your locker inviting you to the party of the year by the most popular guy in school.

The note reads, "I think you are a very nice and beautiful person. I would love to get to know you. Come to my party, and you will be the center of attention."

True Thoughts

Now, imagine that you are the receiver of the note.

1) What would be your natural feeling after receiving that note in your locker?

2) What would be your natural feeling after reading the item found in your locker?

Identifying Scenario, Author Reaction

In this scenario, my first instinctive feeling would be fear and anxiety. I receive a strange note in my locker. I don't know if it is bad news or good. I'm wondering who placed the note in my locker and why. After I read it, I would probably feel a sense of happiness and pleasure. I received a not from a popular person in school, and he would like to make me the focal point of their attention.

Identifying Scenario 2 (b)

After reading the note, ridding your mind of all anxieties and fears, you decide to attend the party. How can you pass up the opportunity of a lifetime? Soon, everyone who ridiculed you will envy you.

You arrive at the house and there are so many people at the party. There are people on the porch, on the front lawn, in the house, and in the back of the home. Your note indicates the party started at 9:30 pm and you arrived at 9:15 pm.

You recognize some people and for the most part, people are cordial. Suddenly the person who sent the note recognizes you and invites you into the house.

The individual then confesses the reason you were invited to the party was a dare and part of a joke. The person also states the only way you can stay at the party is to do their homework.

Relatable Mindset

Relate to you being right there in front of the person who authored that note with ill intentions.

1) What is your first natural feeling?

2) Would you choose to hide this emotion? Why, or why not?

Identifying Scenario, Author Reaction

My "real emotions" would be hurt and anger. I would mask my true feelings and choose to smile while walking away. I would not allow this person to see my pain or thrive on my emotions. Thus, my "real emotions" would be sadness and anger; my "counterfeit emotions" are happiness and contentment.

Ready to take several more steps in your healing journey?

Further, in this chapter, we will define and classify eight emotions to help understand the importance of acknowledging our true feelings.

Contentment -vs- Anger

Contentment is "a state of happiness and satisfaction." (dictionaryonline.com)

Naturally, when we are satisfied physically and emotionally, we are satisfied spiritually. When someone or something disrupts our happiness or sense of enjoyment, we may become angry.

Anger "is a strong feeling of annoyance, displeasure or hostility." Both emotions are natural and real feelings that are innate.

Happiness -vs- Sadness

Happiness, is defined by Dictionary Online as "a gratifying and satisfying experience in which a person is in a state of well-being and gladness."

In both scenarios, Tom and Leigh have experienced happiness. Tom was happy while enjoying the game of basketball. Leigh was delighted as she received a party invitation. Both Tom and Leigh are pleased for a moment until feeling *sadness* after the humiliation of bullying.

The opposite of happiness is, of course, sadness. *Sadness* is "associated with grief and discontent and generally caused by sorrow or regret." (Dictionary Online Dictionary)

Tom and Leigh felt the "*real emotions*" of happiness and sadness.

Uncomfort -vs- Pleasure

The feeling of *comfort* is "a state of physical ease and freedom from pain or constraint. When comfort or relief is absent, this feeling is *uncomfort.* (dictionary.com)

Pleasure is "a feeling of happy satisfaction and enjoyment, and entertainment, contrasted with things done out of necessity." (dictionary.com)

In scenario 1, Tom experiences *pleasure and comfort* while watching his favorite sport and engaging with others, thus experiencing uncomfort and sadness as he is made fun of by two male bullies.

In scenario 2, Leigh has the natural instinctive feeling of *comfort* in focusing on her studies and spending time at home. When she learns she is the brunt of a joke, she feels sad and a sense of *uncomfort.*

Courage -vs- Fear

Courage "is the ability to do something that frightens you."
(dictionary.com) *Fear* is an "unpleasant emotion caused by
the belief that someone or something is dangerous and
likely to cause pain, thus perceived as a potential threat."
(dictionary.com)

At times during our real emotions of fear, we must find
courage. The enemy and darkness thrive upon fear. I ran
from people and things that made me afraid.

Identifying Scenario Conclusion Box

Tom chose to ignore the bullies and continued watching the basketball game. A few of Tom's friends happened to overhear the bullies' comments and redirected them in a positive manner. Tom happens to own a local restaurant and invites everyone back for a free slice of pizza and soft drink. Tom chose to show kindness and courage to the bullies. The bullies felt ashamed of what they did and apologized to Tom. Currently, they are employees at Tom's pizzeria shop. The one tormentor (Kevin) and his mother were recently evicted and homeless. The second tormentor (George) was being physically abused by his father. After speaking with Tom and a couple of his friends, who happened to be therapists, Kevin and George, along with Kevin's mother are living in a new apartment that Tom helped get for them. Leigh was afraid but showed courage by thanking the individual for the invitation and offering to tutor him in the library or study hall. Because of Leigh's courage and kindness, the individual (Anthony) agreed and now they are very good friends. He gave her a public apology and confided in her that he did have a crush on her. He had confessed to one of his friends who teased him, so he pretended that inviting her was a joke. Several months later, Anthony and Leigh are dating. Anthony formed a group at the school advocating against bullying.

Comprehension Check Point!

- ✓ We have classified and defined "real emotions" and "counterfeit emotions."

- ✓ Established how they differ.

  - Real emotions are feelings that are instinctive and come naturally.

  - Counterfeit or "masked emotions", are untrue feelings displayed in front of others or *the "other-self."*

Are you ready for additional steps in your healing journey? Let's go, Survivor!

Going forward, in chapter two,

- ✓ We will examine how the lack of embracing our real emotions hinders our relationship with ourselves.

53

✓ We will study how the lack of embracing real emotions affects our ability to know our worth.

✓ We will analyze what or who the "*other-self*"is and how the enemy uses denial of our "real emotions" to separate us from God.

*The denial to pacify the **other self***

I longed to appease my abusers and show kindness to my abusers out of fear. I never knew why my tormentors gained so much pleasure in harming me. My faith and Christian teachings taught me to look the other way when people hurt me. I was instructed if I didn't forgive my tormentors, I would never inherit God Almighty's Kingdom. So, I suppressed my real emotions, and in time grief consumed me. I hated my bullies, abusers, and everyone that enabled their behavior. I could not say this out loud, but The Heavenly Father knew my heart. I acted out because I was victimized, and the monster who hurt me was able to live his life like nothing was wrong.

This aberration was still able to keep his job, family, reputation, and disturbing sense of peace. Nobody told him he would go to hell and suffer for what he did. The "*real emotions*" of *hate* and *contempt* filled my heart that once welcomed and dwelled in *happiness and love*. I became angry at the people that kept the secret. I was angry at him and all of the people who hurt me.

I could not be real with what I was feeling, I could not value my worth, and I could not have a real relationship with Almighty God. I felt hurt by God because He didn't listen or protect me. I talked to Him and begged God to help me. At a young age, I turned my back on God.

These were the coldest years of my life. I began looking in love in all the wrong places and experienced pain from many people.

The lack of embracing our *real emotions* hinders our relationship with ourselves. Because I hid my *true feelings* from people in the world, I felt worthless. The manipulation from the adversary caused people to hurt me by words. I constantly heard that I was too dark, fat, ugly, and dumb. The adversary made me believe that something was wrong with me. He told me that I didn't belong anywhere through others. Understand that negative thoughts stem from the adversary whispering in your ear.

Reflective Thought

In **Matthew 4:1-11**, Jesus was baptized and led into the wilderness to be tempted by the devil. I refer to the devil and bullies as the adversary. Adversary, according to Merriam-Webster.com, is "someone or something that opposes, resists, and is an enemy or opponent."

The adversary taunted and tried to tempt our Lord Jesus. He whispered in his ear about turning a rock into bread and leaping off the edge to prove He was The Son of God.

All the voices telling me no one loved me; were whispers of satan. The ugly actions by people were the actions of satan.

In my darkness, I felt I was at fault for suppressing my real emotions of anger. I felt because I had contempt for those who hurt me, I was evil for not forgiving them. Those were the thoughts in my depression and journey through darkness. Here was one of my spiritual rock bottoms.

How did I emerge from the darkness? I arose from the darkness by looking up and embracing The One, and Only True Light. God never abandoned me, nor did God allow the pain. I realized I never turned away from God. When I turned around, He was still in front of me. I immediately dropped to my knees, sobbing and shouting my hurt and pain. I looked over my life and the lifestyle I was living. I discovered that my search for love; will never be established by man.

In the light, I graduated from the Struthers High School and Mahoning County Joint Vocational School in 1991. My mother and I began our healing journey. I applied to attend Spellman College and was accepted. In our darkness, our bodies are encased with God's love.

Through trials, we will hear the adversary whispering in our ears. When we face opposition, what must we do?

The enemy uses tactics and our emotions to drown us in *depression, guilt, sorrow, unforgiveness, fear, lust, stress, and unaddressed anger.* With the denial of our "*real emotions,*" we become stagnant, sinking into *emotional quicksand.* We cannot hide our *real emotions* because of fear, ego, and the "*other-self.*"

On the surface, I appeared happy and content, while inside, I was sad, bitter, and alone. I did not want the *"other self"* to feel the hurt and pain I went through. I was ashamed of being molested, abused, and bullied.

Forced to keep the secret of my pain, I felt even more ashamed. I thought I had done something wrong. I rebelled as a teen because I was angry and hurt over what happened to me when I was nine years old. The people in the community labeled me. People threw those philosophical stones that hurt my heart, esteem, and soul.

The monster that stole my innocence and trust, he was considered to be an exemplary citizen and man of God. The oddity went to church with his wife and son. He kept a job by working for the school system. Some people appeared to think highly of him. Myself? I was labeled a juvenile delinquent who would be in jail or dead. ***Imagine.*** I had a criminal record and emotional scars. The anomaly had no criminal record. ***Where is the righteousness in all of this?***

So much anger and resentment filled my heart that I began to smoke and drink. I thought through self-medication, my emotional wounds would heal. This is what I said to my ego and *other-self*.

You owe it to yourself to be "**real**" with yourself. Think back to the times in your life when you may have used *counterfeit emotions*.

You have to acknowledge everything behind those closed doors; you don't have to share it to the world. Restoring the broken self-image and mending your broken wounds; thus, finding graceful intimacy. We cannot live in a bubble and take our journeys for granted. Our journeys through and behind closed doors are adventures in life. We shall go through many trials and tribulations in our lives; nonetheless, I can say from my heart to yours that in our storms, we have God. ***Acknowledge our real emotions,***

and embrace our purpose.

Are ready to take some more leaps in your healing journey?

Let's Go, Survivor!

Notes

2

Defining and Working Through Real Emotions

CHAPTER SCRIPTURES

Matthew 4:1-11

UNIT VOCABULARY WORDS

Real emotions	Sadness	Uncomfort
Counterfeit	Happiness	The Other Self
emotions	Fear	Denial
Masks	Courage	Pacify
Anger	Pleasure	
Contentment	Comfort	

Real emotions:

_____

_____

_____

Counterfeit emotions:

_____

_____

_____

Masks:

_____
_____
_____

Anger:

_____
_____
_____

Contentment:

_____
_____
_____

Sadness:

_____
_____
_____

Happiness:

_____
_____
_____

Fear:

Courage:

_____
_____
_____

Pleasure:

_____
_____
_____

Discomfort:

_____
_____
_____

The Other Self:

_____
_____
_____

Denial:

_____
_____
_____

Pacify:

_____
_____
_____

1. How do real emotions and counterfeit or masked
emotions
differ?_____

_____
_____
_____
_____
_____
_____

2. How would both real and counterfeit emotions affect the

other self?

_____
_____
_____
_____
_____
_____

3. How would the lack of embracing your real emotions hinder you in your life?

_____

_____

_____

_____

_____

_____

_____

_____

4. Who uses the tactics in emotions to distract us?

_____ Please explain your answer and include why this entity would have a motive in distracting us from our purpose.

_____

_____

_____

_____

_____

_____

_____

_____

_____

_____

5. Have you ever used masked emotions? Please share your story and take this time to vent.

_____

_____

_____

_____

_____

_____

_____

_____

_____

_____

_____

_____

_____

_____

_____

_____

_____

_____

_____

_____

_____

_____

_____

TRUE OR FALSE

6. _____ People who bully are just naturally mean and are not going through trials and tribulation themselves.

7. _____ Everyone experiences happiness, sadness, anger, calmness, pleasure, fear, etc. these are our instinctive and real emotions.

8. _____ The bullies in the scenario with Tom, were experiencing displaced anger and some emotional problems and issues in their own environment.

9. _____ You have the right to be real with yourself. Being real with you will build the bridge to knowing your worth.

3

The Hopeless Hinders

Congratulations!

You are more than a quarter of the way on your journey to healing.

We have discussed what can hinder our ability to know our worth and relationship with ourselves, Almighty God, and others. You and I have defined and classified what *"real" and "counterfeit" emotions* are and established how they both differ.

In chapter 1, we learned about how our real instinctive feelings can drain you and me mentally, leading us into *emotional quicksand*.

What you and I haven't discussed are the *hopeless hinders*. *Hopeless hinders* aid in the disconnection of knowing our worth and achieving our purpose in life. You and I were born with the instinctive need to be loved, fed, protected, and nourished. When our natural-born needs are neglected, we experience *real emotions* such as fear, uncomfort, sadness, and anger.

Consider the scripture, **Luke 6:31 (KJV),** "Do unto others as you would want them to do unto you?"

I love this command by God even as a child. I have implanted it within my heart and soul. I wanted to be loved and treated like a human being, and I also loved to treat others with respect. I wanted a roof over my head and food to eat. I longed to feel protected, loved, and have a sense of belonging. I did not want to be homeless, hungry, abused, hated, despised, or alienated.

Reflective Questions

- ❓ If someone hurt you, would you have the instinct to hurt them back, or would you show kindness and hope they change?

- ❓ If you constantly showed compassion and sympathy to those who hurt you, would you fault yourself and allow the continued mistreatment, or would you fault them?

- ❓ If you did fault them, would you remove yourself from the environment and situation, or would you stay in that situation?

Hopelessness hinders are when we internalize someone else's wrongdoing and abuse. We choose to take on someone else's actions and mask our *real emotions* in how we truly feel. *Running from your fears, unaddressed anger, depression, and unforgiveness* are *hopeless hinders*.

In this chapter, we are going to **face our fears head-on!**

Get ready to *address your anger, dig your way out of depression, channel forgiveness, discover coping strategies under stress, and focus on your strengths.*

Running from Your Fears?

I remember in elementary school, afraid to go outdoors during recess because my bullies would torment me. The doors opened, and I saw my group of tormentors waiting for me. My stomach felt so upset. My peers moved at such a fast speed, while I moved at a slow pace.

Just a little over nine years old and my mother had to work. My mother's friend offered to babysit my sister and me. She had a husband who was well respected and worked for the school system. He and his wife appeared to be that loving couple in public and adored their son.

Behind closed doors, he and his wife were monsters that wore masks outdoors. At this moment I no longer had to look underneath my bed or in closets for the boogeyman.

Fear is not something that you or I conjure up out of our heads to gain sympathy or attention. *"Fear* is from a potential threat, an unwelcomed experience, a protector shield to ward off possible dangers;" (dictionary.com) *fear can also be a prison and substance from the emotional quicksand that submerges someone into depression.*

I began inventing sicknesses and excuses to go to school. I began throwing tantrums when it was time to go to certain babysitters' homes. Please parents pay attention to your children and listen to what they tell you and watch their behaviors and actions.

As I grew older, I began dating all the wrong men. I allowed *fear* to drive me to men who I thought would be able to protect me and be a father figure for me. At the age of fifteen, I was in my first domestic violence relationship. Not all of my relationships were violent. Not all of my relationships were physical abuse either. There is emotional, verbal, and mental abuse as well. What made me stay in some of those relationships? ***The answer is fear.***

There were two types of fears that kept me in those dim relationships.

The first set of fear was *egocentric worries*. *Egocentrism,* according to the Oxford Languages Online Dictionary, is "thinking only of oneself, without regard for the feelings or desires of others; self-centered."

My abuser thought only of himself by oppressing me through violence or words. I stayed because I thought of myself when it came to the fear of being out of a relationship, not being sexually pleased, not having him help me financially, or giving me that honeymoon attention after the abuse. Yes, in some situations I looked for gifts after the storm. I knew the worse he treated me; the bigger the gift.

The other set of fears were the *submissive or compliant fears*. To be *submissive* is " inclined or ready to submit or yield to the authority of another; unresistingly or humbly obedient:" (dictionary.com)

Compliance is "the act or process of complying (yielding) to a desire, demand, proposal, or regimen or coercion (pressure, force, or intimidation). (Merriam-webster.com)

My *compliant fears* were <u>death, harm to myself and my children, homelessness, and hurting him by leaving.</u>

I reflect on my life and I think of the places I chose not to go because of fear.

At the age of forty-five, I am finding courage in the face of all my adversities. I prayed after my divorce that I would be able to love again and trust men; however, the hopeless hinder of running from my fears has kept me from loving and trusting another man. We have to know that fear is not of God, Power, or Love. Fear is the work of the enemy to weaken our drive to achieve our purpose in life and draw us into the darkness of *unaddressed anger.*

FEAR IS . . .
NOT OF POWER
NOT OF LOVE

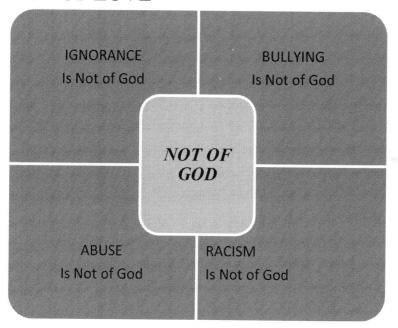

IGNORANCE
Is Not of God

BULLYING
Is Not of God

NOT OF GOD

ABUSE
Is Not of God

RACISM
Is Not of God

FEAR IS . . .
OF WEAKNESS &
THE IDLE WORK OF THE ENEMY

When people are unkind, it is because they lack love for themselves.

Unkind and abusive people are dealing with inner fear. The only entity that lives in fear is the enemy because he knows his days are numbered. **Revelation 20:13-15**

Unaddressed Anger?

Fear and anger parallel at times. The combination of emotions, and frustration, provides a perfect storm for unaddressed feelings. *Malicious gossiping, domestic violence, and physical, emotional, and verbal abuse* to name only a few are heinous acts, which I believe, are out of *unaddressed anger* and or fear.

When there is a failure to acknowledge your *real emotions*, the storm brews. In life, there will always be night and day, darkness and light, good and evil. The tormentors will always look for a victim; the victim may be drawn to that tormented soul. To ensure we heal from our traumatic experiences, we must address the plausibility of the environment.

- ✓ Some men or women may abuse their spouse or significant other because of fear.

- ✓ Some women or men may stay in an abusive relationship out of fear.
- ✓ Some men or women may abuse because of their unaddressed anger.
- ✓ Some people experience depression when their anger is turned inward.
- ✓ Some people may experience anxiety when their anger and fear are not addressed.

Explanation, I have spoken about my younger days of being bullied. We all agree that there was an eminent fear that I had to go to school. However, there was another real emotion that I did not reveal. I would lie if I told you that I never became angry at them. I was so angry and bitter at my tormentors for hurting me. I would never hurt them the way they are hurting me. I had a strong disliking towards them and later I came to understand as an adult, I had turned my anger inward. My *anger* was the *hopeless hinder*, called DEPRESSION.

Depression is defined by the online dictionary as, "feelings of severe despondency (hopelessness, or misery) and dejection (sadness)." Mayo Clinic further explains, "That *depression* is a mental health disorder characterized by persistently depressed mood or loss of interest in activities, causing significant impairment in daily life."

I wasn't motivated to either wake up in the morning or go through my daily activities. I felt as though I were going through the motions of being alive. I only found comfort in my sleep or my uninterrupted dreams.

I lost my interest in writing. I stopped going to church and spending time with my family. My spirituality was diminished by the darkness (so I thought). In this darkness, my pain was a philosophical grave. I was genially hurt but I did not acknowledge or address my anger. I thought to myself, that if I dared to say I hated my enemies, I would be punished by God. Through My failure to acknowledge and address my true feelings, I punished myself.

In hating my adversaries, I was just as ignorant and bad as they were.

I tried to mask my *real emotions* of <u>contempt with sadness.</u> I would pretend to forgive my abusers. *Behind the closed doors in my heart,* I wished for their demise. Almighty God knew my heart and the truth. We can never be counterfeit or dishonest with God.

Bullying played an obstacle in my life. As an adult, I experience cognitive delays and feelings of inadequacy. "Students who are bullied, are more likely to experience low self-esteem and isolation. Bullied students also perform poorly in school, have few friends, and have a negative view of the school. As I shared earlier, I became ill when tormented. Students who are taunted tend to experience physical symptoms such as headaches, stomachaches, problems sleeping, and experienced mental health issues. Mental health issues include but are not limited to: depression, suicidal thoughts, and anxiety." (The

Center for Disease Control, Bullying Surveillance among Youths, 2014)

I began isolating myself, overeating more and more, and acting out. I was disruptive in church. Around the age of nine and ten, I bullied people.

Thankfully, my mother and grandmother intervened. I could have become a tyrant just like my hectors. But the Heavenly Father knew it would have altered my stitching. God blessed me with a grandmother and mother who were not going to allow this.

I was angry, hurt, bitter, and afraid. However, at a young age, I was taught because someone hurt you; does not give you the right to hurt anyone else. I was taught right from wrong. I was taught not to bully or abuse.

The bullying continued from others, I dealt with my real emotions of anger and pain by suppressing it inward. As an adolescent, I began acting out again out of pain. I remember people shouting and asking me, "what is wrong with you? Why are you so angry?" My heart was so heavy and pained, that I couldn't give an answer.

- ! I was angry that I was victimized.
- ! I despised my body.
- ! I hated eating out of boredom and misery.
- ! I felt ugly and wanted to feel beautiful.

Just a little over fifteen years of age, I began several different relationships. In my first relationship, I was a sophomore in high school and he was a senior. This was my first domestic violent relationship. He and I broke up about a year later, and it was then I dated men. <u>My promiscuous behavior began because of my disposition to embrace forgiveness and knowledge of my worth.</u>

I loathed my body and I gave it away for free because I felt I was worthless. *The mental and philosophical plantation of random procreation and promiscuity.*

I became so enraged in life at my bullies, my situations, and my memories. The memory of my biological father who abandoned me. The memory of the only father I knew, my grandfather, passed away just one day after my birthday on December 23, 1984.

My mother was an industrious worker and had to make choices to provide for my sister and me. I faulted her for the things in my life. I used to seethe when people scolded me for my rebellious behavior. "Why are you so disobedient towards your mother?" They would yell. "You have such a good mother, why don't you listen to her?" Another would blurt.

I never acknowledged them with an answer by words; I answered through my actions of disrespect. My actions were the spoken expressions of my real emotions. I felt my mother left me in the hands of my tormentor because she chose her job over me. As an adult I know now this wasn't the case. However, as a child, I thought differently. Because of my obstacles, I have trust issues which impeded many avenues in my life. I had problems making and keeping friends because I had no trust. I had no love for myself, and I felt I turned my back on God. My life was just ridiculous, and I continued dating all the wrong men.

In my senior year in high school, I had another spiritual epiphany. I thought to myself, "no more bullying, I could start my life over free from negative people." I began studying with Jehovah's Witness' and I thought all of my hectoring days were over. I thought at this point I can put the blocks of sadness behind me and enjoy life.

In 1992, I met my ex-husband who swept me off my feet. He was different from any guy I had dated. He was polite and charming, he would send flowers, and he didn't initiate having sex on the first date. In 1993, we were married, and a little over one year later, I gave birth to our son, Patrick.

It was during my pregnancy with our first child that I remember the first time he hit me.

That hit was the most shocking, hurtful, fearful, and angry moment of my life.

I was carrying his child and he promised he would never hurt me.

Shockingly, I forgave him and we had more children. There were countless other strikes, punches, kicks, and chokes while I carried his children inside of me.

There were times I prayed for God to take me.

In the Douglass household, the *real emotions* of *fear and anger* were a philosophical boxing ring.

I was so confused, I felt alone. I thought, "how can this man love me and his children; yet, he shows so much hate?" I pondered, "how can people confess to being Christians when they judge me for staying in a relationship which they know nothing about?"

The National Coalition against Domestic Violence documents corroborates, "Domestic violence is the leading cause of injury to women than car accidents, muggings and rapes combined. Every nine seconds in the United States of America, a woman is assaulted or beaten. In the United

States of America, alone people who suffer from domestic violence, lose nearly 8 million days of paid work per year. This is equivalent to 32,000 full-time jobs."

What you have gone through in life, isn't meant to destroy or consume you.

What you went through is to build you up and make you stronger.

I was verbally, emotionally, and physically abused; now, I can be a voice and example of healing and strength. If I did not endure those hardships, I could not minister nor help any of you. *You are the torches of light that will go forward and help others.*

I was molested, raped, stalked, talked about, violated, and bullied. *Now, I am a whole survivor unable to be broken down by man.*

We are God's beautifully designed vases. Although we are fragile; *we are not weak*. Situations in life may cause us to break, and over time the pieces of that vase may become harder to place back together. Nevertheless, "we are beautifully broken" and able to mend through our Christ Jesus. (Cece Winans)

I understand now the reasoning for my struggles. I understand my purpose in life. The loss of my grandfather, grandmother, and daughter are memories I hold close to my heart and strengthen me to do good. I will see them again one morning. This manual and book are a reflection of them.

I was told to forgive my tormentors, I was told to get out of domestic abuse situations, and I was told to heal; however, I never was told how. This is my reason for writing this book.

I share my struggles, giving a guide that was not given to me. *I had to focus on my strengths and be honest with my* real emotions. I had to focus on what meant the most to me in my life and my children. If it were not for my children and God, I would have been gone long ago.

I reached that point in my life where I knew my children deserved more.

I had so many trust issues and I feared dark places, hallways, and large groups of people. Not so long-ago people spoke about my fear of large groups of people and isolation. I never was vocal about my truth behind closed doors until recently. *I was not born to fear; fear was born to me.*

I had to learn that situations and some people impregnated me with fear, and *I chose to give birth to fear.* Now, *I have the power of choice to discipline fear and correct it.*

You Have Rights

- ✓ You have the right to your natural feelings!
- ✓ You have the right to express how you feel!

- ✓ You have the right to set boundaries!

- ✓ You have the right to say "NO!"

- ✓ You have the right to seek justice for being wronged!

- ✓ You have the right to heal!

Alright Survivor, take another leap in your healing journey!

God is not going to punish anyone for being honest in how they feel.

When you suppress your real emotions, unaddressed feelings are birthed, and negative expressions are displayed.

I owed a loving and safe home for my children, free from debauchery and chaos.

Yes, fear and anger kept me in this domestic violent relationship. Fear, anger, and the failure of acknowledging my *real emotions* kept me from growing spiritually and emotionally. Deep down inside I was angry that my baby passed and I was angry at The Lord. I had to be honest that I faulted my trials and tribulations with being homeless and unable to keep a stable job.

I feel that if certain things did not happen to me, I would have graduated from college, and gainfully employed. Yes, I suffered from that entitlement perspective. I felt the world owed me for my misery. Today, I can say that everything I went through made me perfectly seasoned, and I owe God everything.

KNOW,

FEAR AND ANGER ARE NOT OF

POWER NOR ARE THEYOF LOVE

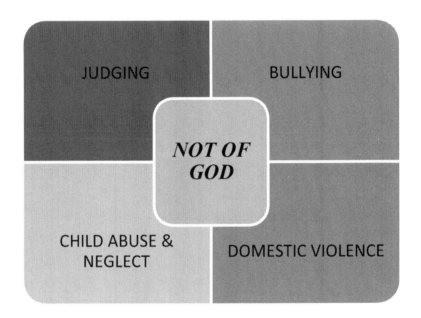

THESE ARE EMOTIONS OF ANXIETY

THE IDLE WORK OF THE ENEMY,

TRYING TO DIM YOUR LIGHT

Channeling Forgiveness

After the storm, acknowledgment of your *real emotions*, and *addressing your unresolved true feelings*, *you can channel true forgiveness.*

The fact is, you cannot forgive anyone when you refuse to acknowledge the wrong or injustice.

Consider

- ? How can you open the doors to the world when you refuse to unlock them?

- ? How can you excuse someone, when you won't acknowledge the crime or offense, they have committed against you?

This pivotal point in your journey will be the most rewarding.

- ✓ In this section, we shall arise from the emotional quicksand that has deceived us.
- ✓ In this section, we go behind the doors of our hearts and souls to further embrace our real emotions and address our hopeless hinders to channel forgiveness.

The Journey of Thought Process to Forgiveness

- Today, I can forgive my tormentors and abusers because I can honestly say I had anger toward them. I can say honestly, that I despised them and their actions.
- Today, I can differentiate between them and their actions enabling me to forgive the person and not the action.

You can never undo the wrong, you can apologize or forgive the person. The wrong action can never be right in the eyes of God; however, the person can be forgiven in the eyes of God. *Remember, people are forgiven not the actions.*

To say this aloud without fear of judgment is the best empowerment I have ever felt. To break the silence, I have healing that no person can take away from me. I can be honest with God about my true feelings in how I felt about my daughter's passing. I don't have to mask my hurt and pain anymore.

I forgive my ex-husband for what he did to me and our children. This is your journey and time to celebrate what you choose to forgive.

Survivor, who and why do you choose to forgive them at this moment?

Another Leap Through a Healing Exercise

- On a piece of paper, or in a journal, write down who and what you choose to forgive.
- Then write the reason why you are forgiving them.

Once you have healed your inner peace and channeled forgiveness, you become whole. There will be more hardships. There will be people who will mock you. Yes, even to date people try to test my faith and patience. However, by being honest with the way I am feeling, I convey my real emotions professionally and firmly.

No one has the right to make you feel unhappy, less intelligent, less attractive, or less important. It is alright to be angry when losing a loved one. It is alright to tell God how you feel and why you feel that way. Our God created us and He knows **_EXACTLY_** how we feel.

You have the right to your natural feelings and when those emotions are addressed, our actions can be positively and professionally defined.

Meditative Questions

1) When you were wronged, what were your real emotions?

2) Did you suppress your real emotions at the time?

       a. Why or why not?

3) Can you or do you forgive them?

       a. Please explain.

Meditation Activity

Tres Luces meaning "Three Lights"

For this exercise you will need to purchase three candles.

You will choose a [1]candle of your favorite color, [2]a white candle, and [3]a purple or lavender candle.

[1]While lighting the [A] purple or [B] lavender candle, you will begin acknowledge what and who has hurt you in life.
Out loud you will say, *"When you,* the individual's name, state the crime they committed against you. *I felt* state how they made you feel.
I wanted you to state what you wanted them not to do or what you wanted them to do."

State how they affected your life and what you think they should do now.

Feel free to vent as you see all of your pain and frustration going in flame.

[2]When *YOU* have shared all of your grief and pain you will light the [C] white candle. This is ***the forgiveness candle.***
Out loud you will say, *"I forgive you* the individual's name, *for* state what you are forgiving them for and why. *My* state your real emotion in how they made you feel. The feeling(s) of state your feelings again *shall burn and become no more. I am free from your hurt and pain.*

[3]Then you will light the third candle (color of your choice) which is your candle, the candle of **self-empowerment**. You will state how you will take control of your destiny.

You will state how no one has the right to hurt or harm you anymore.

You can also share your goals and aspirations.

These exercises feel free to do daily and whenever you need to. Forgiveness isn't instant; it takes time.

Digging Out of Depression

Addressing Long-Term Effects from Trauma

It is time you embrace your worth and understand that you have undergone trials and tribulations because you are highly favored. The enemy has no power over you or your mind. Because you shine bright, the adversary will taunt you. However, you have the strength to overcome the hardships. I have struggled with depression and Post Traumatic Stress Disorder (PTSD) throughout my life.

At times I had no drive to get out of bed or interact with my children. *I would keep the shades drawn and the lights out because* **darkness was my cave.**

After overcoming great storms in our lives, there will be the aftermath. I learned that healing isn't spontaneous; healing is a part of your everyday life. My children are my God-given lifelines in this world, and one child I feel was stolen from me by death. My third-born Kailah passed away in 1998. I knew of the spirit of death but never personally like this.

The next year my grandmother passed away.

If it were not for my two eldest children, and my youngest son, I wouldn't be here today.

Survivors, storms will come one after another, and healing is an everyday pursuit. At times we feel sad, hopeless, and powerless. These feelings are sometimes referred to as a *depression*. I had to understand how to channel myself to forgive and dig my way out of depression. *Depression* is the very foundation of *emotional quicksand.*

If I stayed in that turbulent relationship, my children and I would sink. *I decided that our positive energy and matter could no longer be mixed or watered down by his hate.* ***We deserved to be safe and at peace.***

With the loss of my daughter and the birth of my youngest son, I knew my children deserved more. I made the conscious decision to leave our abuser (my ex-husband and children's father). Just as Jochebed (Moses' mother) chose to bring her infant son to safety; I chose to flee with God's speed with my children. (Exodus 2:1-10)

I contacted the local domestic violence organization by the name of AWARE, and we were free. The agency helped with my divorce. My children and I could start a new life in safety.

The storm was over; however, there was the aftermath.

Depression and anxiety still had their chains on my mind, spirit, and soul. My children experienced emotional problems because of what they endured. It took years of counseling and years of putting the pieces back together. I thought my hardships were behind me and I enrolled at Youngstown State University.

I felt I was on the road to productivity, prosperity, and good old resilience. I majored in Social Work because I knew I endured so much and would help others. I knew that a child acting out and in trouble may have gone through a storm behind their closed doors. I knew that a woman that appears to be confused and indecisive may not be immature or telling untruths; she may be a victim of abuse. I had plans to get my Bachelor's degree and obtain my Master's in Counseling. I knew one day I would be able to help someone go through the same or similar storms I endured. I knew my hardships were not in vain.

Then the vase was dropped again.

Approximately three years into school I had a stalker. Over several months he made our (my children, my mother, and sister) lives a living hell. This ordeal was the second hardest storm of my life. However, this time I was able to acknowledge and address my real emotions.

I knew I couldn't throw everything away by seeking vengeance. In surviving all of the other storms, I knew I could survive this squall too.

I promised my daughter and God that I would live my life to inherit God's Kingdom. (Luke 22:25:30, Revelation 21:3-7)

For the first time in my life, I felt alive. I had no fear of large crowds or attending my local university. I was at a spiritual high in my life. Nonetheless, I was knocked down by oppression again. I recall at times not knowing how or if I would survive this storm.

The ill spirit of depression made itself known again. My curtains opened every morning to the sunrise and were now closed to the darkness within my soul again.

Depression, which I refer to as the *vampire disease*, began a dark love affair. Depression would entice me with a tender kiss upon my cheek and soon suck the life from my very lips. Within moments I would lay on my side, unable to move and breathe. I recall going to the local prosecutor's office as my tormentor made allegations against me, thinking I would never survive this ordeal. A lady affirmed that this storm would end. Surprisingly, the storm departed.

It took a big chunk out of my soul; however, with the grace of God, I was healed.

Survivors, you have to remember in life, you will have challenges. Those challenges will help you grow!

After each storm, my shine became brighter, my skin thicker, and my heart much bigger.

Depression is a monster, an oppressor, and a friend to emotional quicksand. Speak over yourself and against those invisible hectors.

In 2012, I opened my business Wilson & Clark Independent General Contracting Services LLC (WCD Professional Services LLC.) On May 14, 2014, I graduated from Youngstown State with my Associate's degree in social work. January 1, 2018, I founded my non-profit organization, Behind Closed Doors Ministries LLC.

After the spiritual warfare, there will be the aftermath. For every aftermath, there will be new art to share.

Survivor, I share my past with you to help myself and you. This healing journey is a continuous road. Each day we learn something new. The key to healing and restoring your inner peace is the power of choice within you. Vases our fragile and must be handled with care.

Because I denied my real emotions and failed to acknowledge my fears, I became disconnected from my children and the world around me.

In 2016, I went through the storm of wrongful termination. I was a front desk clerk, and the prior owners sold the hotel. Within a few months, due to bias, and prejudice, my position with the hotel was no more.

The Vase, Dropped AGAIN!

I withdrew from the roles as a mother, daughter, sister, and friend. I was officially a failure in my mind.

My children began to tell me that they missed me. I was physically in my home; however, I was spiritually someplace else. My daughter told me she missed the way I played gospel music. My youngest son said he missed his old mom. My oldest son would continuously ask if I were alright.

I would sneak off into the bathroom or my bedroom to cry.

Slowly, I died inside. I slept by day and lived at night. I despised the sunlight; my children had their nights and days confused. It was so hard to change this as they got older and had to go to school. My depression took a lot of happiness from my life. It wasn't until I embraced my _real emotions, emerged from the emotional quicksand, addressed these hopeless hinders, and channeled forgiveness,_ that I dug my way out of depression.

I cried like never before as I called out to Almighty God. I shouted my real emotions against the creature that molested me. I cried out about despising him for what he did to my sister, myself, and another young girl. I told God how hurt and angry I was at Him for allowing it to happen. I continued to vent with our Heavenly Father about other frustrations I had. I hurt that my baby left before me. I detested my husband for raping me and beating our children. Every emotion, hurt, and pain I let out of my mouth.

Then I felt the heaviness of burdens and grief leave my body. I cried myself to sleep and felt The Lord's Arms comforting me. When I woke, I took a long hot bath and wept again.

I told my children I loved them, and I cooked dinner for the first time in a long time.

I called my dear friends, whom I call my sisters. They encouraged me to share my story on Facebook. Arlesa Ferguson of Diverse Resolutions interviewed me, and later I shared my live broadcasts documenting my journey, entitled MCD Journey through Opened Doors. Through each segment, I felt a healing and change.

Survivor, it is time to write your success story in your journey. What you went through is the writing in your book.

To further the distance in your survival journey, I would like to share some additional strategies that helped me.

I learned that you have to rest when you endure hardships or gain significant understanding. Consider that you are studying for a final exam or you disagreed with someone that emotionally drained you; you are overwhelmed and tired. What you need now is rest.

When organizing a local Bible study group in the community, I implemented the concept and need for **R.E.S.T.** into my daily living.

R.E.S.T. is the acronym that stands for Recognizing, Encouraging, Strengthen/Strive, and Team building.

- **R:**
  - Recognizing things that trigger your depression and recognizing your symptoms that indicate you are depressed.

- **E:**

  - Encourage yourself and those living with depression that **"this too shall pass." Things will become better. We are normal. We will get through this.**

- **S:**

  - Strengthen yourself physically, spiritually and emotionally.

  - Focus on your STRENGTHS!

  - Take time to think about what you like to do.

    - What are your hobbies that take you out of your unhappy place?

- **T:**

  - Team building!

    - ✓ Build your team of prayer warriors, encouragers, and a support team.

✓ Only surround yourself with positive people and energy!

✓ It takes The Almighty God, time, tools, and a positive team to help restore and keep your inner peace!

The only way to dig your way out of depression is to remove the bulk of perceptions. Hand over the sandbags of real emotions mixed with your sorrow and resentment. Draw open the shades, open the doors and restore your happiness and peace.

Each day will be another expedition. Each journey in life will bring you more empowerment, wisdom, and peace.

Yes, there will be difficult times, yet you have the power to survive and thrive. The enemy will continuously try to taunt the brightest of lights. He will use others to try and dim your light. The antagonist has no power over you, your home, spirit, or mind.

Here are additional strategies for preparing yourself as a lifetime survivor of traumatic experiences.

✓ Prepare yourselves for all spiritual warfare.

○ When there is a chance of rain, you carry an umbrella.

○ When there is a possible thunderstorm, you have candles and flashlights by your side.

✓ It is time to recognize the triggers and symptoms that bring on your storm of depression.

o For example, arguments and fights bring on my anxiety. After a disagreement, I'm exhausted emotionally and physically.

✓ I focus on things that make me feel happy and give me a sense of empowerment.

o When you focus on your strengths, you will draw close to who you are and your purpose.

✓ Build up your team of supporters.

✓ Surround yourself with the circle of light that will encourage, nurture, protect, and love you through the rain and shine.

Coping Strategies under Stress

The next thing I would like to cover is a few coping strategies when faced with stressors in your life. We are preparing ourselves for spiritual battles.

People will try to provoke you into anger or steer you into depression. Whenever I am under attack, I think of a calm place. I empathize that this person is going through a storm too. Perhaps, my light can be the beacon to guide them to spiritual change. I focus on my goals and what I want to achieve in life. I will not allow the enemy to deplete my spiritual wealth.

Daily prayer and meditation are the keys to restoration and healing. Tr*es luces* (three lights) meditation is something I invented to overcome my trials and tribulations. This exercise helped me see my hurt inflamed, enabling me to channel peace.

**Survivor,** [1]you will begin by lighting the purple or lavender candle while stating who and or what has hurt you in life. [2]Next, you will take the white candle (forgiveness candle) and light this candle, stating the name of who harmed you and how this person hurt you. [3]The third candle is your self-empowerment torch. Choose your favorite color for this candle.

Declare how you will take control of your destiny. Declare how no one has the right to hurt or harm you anymore.

✓ Whatever brings you from a state of uncomfort to comfort, this will be a coping strategy.

✓ Whatever brings you from the emotion of sadness to happiness, this will be your coping strategy. If you enjoy singing, dancing, writing, speaking, designing, and acting, allow those God-given talents to bring you to freedom!

✓ If you desire higher education and advancement, achieve your way to freedom! Allow your strengths to be your coping skills!

Finding Focus

As the hail beats against your body, the wounds sustained are deep and pained. When the wind blows your spirit in every direction, you become emotionally drained. When the furious waters settle, your body and spirit lay dormant in the aftermath. The Heavenly Father tells you to get up, and He takes you in His Arms. All those philosophical shattered glasses that cut you deep begin to heal.

To find focus, I had to seek closure. I had to seek happiness knowing with everything I went through; I was still here on earth. *I am alive.* God, I love and thank You for allowing me to be seasoned, tenderized, broken, and healed.

Survivors, there are things we have to acknowledge and accept in this journey called life.

■ We will go through struggles.

■ People will hurt and offend us.

We will be lied to, called names, tested, and tried.

In the midst of these trials, our light will forever shine.

My focus is to share my testimony and be that beacon of light for others that have gone through hardship. To all mothers, focus on your children. Our children did not ask to be here. Never put a significant other before your precious children. To all the fathers, focus on your children, for you are the head of the household. No one will love your children the way you do. Take time to teach your sons to be men and your daughters to be princesses.

Abusers, perpetrators, bullies, thieves, molesters, and rapists; focus on change. Even darkness has the ability to become light. Bind your hands and evil thoughts In The Holy Name of Jesus Christ! Focus on change and do what is good in The Eyes of God! In Jesus Christ's Name I Pray, Amen.

May we, the nation, find focus not to judge, hate, and destroy. May we, brothers and sisters, find the focus to be impartial, love, and create.

We will rebuild our hearts, spirits, homes, communities, states, and countries. *Tres Luces*

Notes

3

Hopeless Hinders

UNIT VOCABULARY WORDS

- Hopeless Hinders
- Egocentric fears
- Compliant/submis sive fears
- Depression
- Vampire Disease
- tres luces
- R.E.S.T.
- Forgiveness

Hopeless Hinders:

_____

_____

_____

Egocentric fears:

_____

_____

_____

Compliant/submissive fears:

_____

_____

_____

Depression:

_____
_____
_____
_____
_____

Vampire Disease:

_____
_____
_____

tres luces:

_____
_____
_____

R.E.S.T.:

_____
_____
_____
_____
_____
_____
_____
_____
_____
_____

_____
_____
_____

Forgiveness:

_____
_____
_____
_____

QUESTION & ANSWER SECTION

1. What instinctive needs were we born with?

_____
_____
_____
_____
_____

2. What happens when those instinctive needs are not met?

_____
_____
_____
_____
_____

3. What does Luke 6:31 command?

_____

_____

_____

_____

_____

4. What is a misconception about fear?

_____

_____

_____

_____

_____

5. What is fear?

_____

_____

_____

_____

_____

_____

_____

6. Why may people invent sicknesses or throw tantrums in order to prevent going to school or someone's house?

_____
_____
_____
_____
_____
_____
_____

7. When should intervention from bullying and potential domestic violence or abuse take place?

_____
_____
_____
_____
_____
_____
_____
_____

8. What is, "the vase," the Author refers to as describing her battle with trials and tribulations?

_____
_____
_____
_____

9. Why did the Author choose to write this book?

_____
_____
_____
_____

10. What did the Author have to focus, learn, and realize to
    begin the process of healing and forgiveness?

_____

_____

_____

_____

_____

_____

_____

_____

_____

11. What are some of the reasons people abuse or
    experience anxiety and depression?

_____

_____

_____

_____

_____

_____

12. What are the three rights the Author declares in her
    book?

_____

_____

_____

_____

_____

_____

13. What are the steps in digging your way out of depression?

_____

_____

_____

_____

_____

_____

14. What are the 7 beginning steps listed when coping with stress?

_____

_____

_____

_____

_____

_____

_____

_____

15. Instead of focusing on judging, hating, and destroying others; we should focus on . . .

_____

_____

_____

_____

_____

_____

_____

_____

TRUE OR FALSE

16. _____ With the hopeless hinders we tend not to realize that we internalize our real emotions.

.

17. _____ Regularly the hopeless hinders that you and I deal with are: Running from your fears, unaddressed anger, depression, and unforgiveness.

18. _____ Fear and anger are both emotions that can parallel one another.

19. _____ Students who are bullied are more likely to experience low self-esteem and isolation, perform poorly in school, have few friends in school, have a negative view of school, experience physical symptoms (such as headaches, stomachaches, or problems sleeping), and to experience mental health issues (such as depression, suicidal thoughts, and anxiety).

20. _____ You cannot teach someone not to hit when you hit them.

21. _____ You cannot make someone conform to what your beliefs are by oppression.

22. _____ Domestic violence is not the leading cause of injury to women.

23. _____ Every 9 seconds in the US a woman is assaulted or beaten.

24. _____ In the United States of America alone people who suffer from domestic violence loses nearly 8 million days of paid work per year. This is equivalent to 32,000 full-time jobs.

25. _____ To remove the bulk of perceptions you must: a) hand over the sandbags of real emotions that have been mixed with your sorrow and resentment. b) Draw open, the shades and open the doors to your real emotions and address the hopeless hinders.

26. _____ The enemy will not continuously try to taunt and trick you.

27. _____ The enemy will not try and use others to

dim your light.

4

Loving Yourself (The Priceless Rights)

Yo have the right to say no and, in your life, set boundaries. You also have the right to be unharmed, and if anyone should violate your priceless rights, you also have the right to tell.

You are a priceless gift; know your worth. Like a diamond, you are strong and unable to break.

The enemy will try to cut you and dim your shine. However, like a diamond, you may be scuffed and accumulate sand. In the end, our Heavenly Father shall buff and wipe you clean.

No one will love you like our Heavenly Father and King of all kings. We are imperfect people serving a perfect God. Every single person walking this earth will go through their storms. What we learn and do within our bombardments separates us from the darkness of those storms. *You are a priceless gem with priceless rights. Love yourself because you are your priceless receipt.*

The enemy will work through people to cause you grief. Whenever you and I experience negativity from the world, we have removed ourselves from that pleasant place and forget to focus on our goals. We must focus on our coping strategies. Remember, you deserve happiness, peace, and a relationship with yourself.

Take time to take yourself out to the movies, dinner, a suite at the hotel, or a few moments to read a good book. Take time out daily to have a conversation with the LORD. *With daily prayer and meditation, you begin to understand your likes and dislikes, establish boundaries, and set goals in your life.*

You and I know that the enemy works through people to dissuade you from happiness and accomplishing your

139

purpose. The adversary will try to deter you by placing invisible price tags on you. Your worth is non-negotiable; you are priceless. Every day you have a journey to take and will be trialed. No more shall you dwell in worry of facing your fears.

Survivor, if you cannot be honest with yourself and true to your feelings, you will not be genuine to anyone.

Your real emotions will always exist, **Behind Closed Doors** in our homes and our hearts. Acknowledge your true feelings or emotions and refuse to wear the mask of perceptions again. ***There is nothing to be ashamed of for someone else's crimes. You have the right to be unharmed, and if anyone should violate that right, you have the right to tell. Telling is good.***

Survivors on these final steps to healing on this journey, we learn freedom. We are free to tell and acknowledge our true feelings and emotions. We hand over our bags of sand to Almighty God.

With the denial of our real emotions, we become stagnant and sink into that emotional quicksand.

I was angry that my baby had passed. I had to be honest that I faulted my trials and tribulations on my mother, bullies, and some of my family. I had to cast away the entitlement philosophy; no one owed me anything. *Today, I can say that everything I went through made me perfectly seasoned and restored.*

We cannot hide our real emotions because of fear or ego, the other self. Quicksand can only form when the water is added to its substance. We are not going to give the enemy any additions to our substance. **Romans 8:6 (KJV)** "6 For to be carnally minded is death, but to be spiritually minded is life and peace." I have learned that I am a priceless gem shining brightly.

Survivors, you are shining like the midnight star. It is time that you reach within and tell the world what you have endured. With our testimonies, we gain power over darkness. It is time for our oppressors to take accountability, so saith The LORD.

Those hopeless hinders have no power against our Sovereign LORD. Because someone has harmed you or me, we won't keep THEIR lie in secrecy. We are not going to internalize someone's wrongdoing and abuse. We will NOT take on a person's actions nor wear THEIR masks. No more shall we run from happiness or live in fear. There are no monsters hidden underneath our beds. No longer will we be consumed or ignore our anger. If there is unaddressed anger that we are dealing with, we will seek professional help to address it positively.

You and I will no longer be a slave to the vampire disease called; depression.

Unforgiveness and bitterness will no more be the chains that oppress you and me. In restoring your inner peace, you cross the bridge of truth and accountability. The injustices forced against you and me are not our debt nor our fault.

Continue to embrace your worth, and understand that you have undergone trials and tribulations because you are highly favored. The enemy has no power over you or your mind. We cannot make abusers change. ***Abusers need help, and by telling, we aid the winds of truth to reveal the wrong.***

Survivors, your journey in restoring your inner peace is complete. It is time to reopen your hearts and minds to freedom from bitterness and pain. Open your curtains and embrace the sunlight. The enemy has no power over you, your home, or your spirit.

Recognize your triggers and symptoms that bring your depression on and know your *Priceless Rights.* You have the right to say no, and set boundaries. You have the right to be unharmed, and if anyone should violate your priceless rights, you also have the right to tell.

We, the nation, shall find focus not to judge, hate, and destroy. My brothers and sisters, you and I shall uncover a direction to be impartial, love, and create. United you and I will rebuild our hearts, spirits, homes, communities, states, and countries. *Tres Luces*

Priceless Rights

You Have the Right to Say No!

You Have the Right to Set Boundaries!

You Have the Right to Be Unharmed!

YOU HAVE THE RIGHT TO **TELL**!!!

Anyone who violates your priceless rights, TELL.

You are a priceless gift and shall know your worth.

Like a diamond, you are strong and unable to break.

The enemy will try to cut you and dim your shine,

> but like a diamond you may be scuffed and collect sand.

In the end, our Heavenly Father shall buff and wipe you clean.

"Each day will be a journey; it is not easy when you are favored by God." -Michelle Carter-Douglass

Tres Luces Commitment

We, the nation, shall find focus not to judge, hate, and destroy. My brothers and sisters, you and I shall uncover a direction to be impartial, love, and create. United you and I will rebuild our hearts, spirits, homes, communities, states, and countries. ***Tres Luces***

4

Loving Yourself (The Priceless Rights)

UNIT VOCABULARY WORDS

The Priceless Rights   Tres Luces Commitment

The Priceless Rights:

_____

_____

_____

_____

_____

_____

_____

Tres Luces Commitment:

_____

_____

_____

_____

_____

_____

1. What do you deserve in life and what are some ways to go about accomplishing this?

    _____

    _____

    _____

    _____

_____

_____

2. What are two reasons why it is time that you should
   reach within and tell the world what you have endured?

_____

_____

_____

_____

_____

_____

3. What is an example of how the enemy will try dimming
   your light and what are two examples given in the
   chapter that we can do in the face of opposition?

_____

_____

_____

_____

_____

_____

_____

_____

_____

TRUE OR FALSE

4. _____ No one will love you like our Heavenly Father and King of all kings.

5. _____ Not everyone goes through individual storms and experiences trials and tribulations.

6. _____ Only some people are priceless.

7. _____ Those hopeless hinders have no power against our Sovereign LORD.

8. _____ Because someone has harmed you we do NOT have to keep THEIR secrecy.

GLOSSARY

Anger:
Anger is a strong feeling or annoyance, displeasure of hostility.

Bottomless:
Having no foundation or bottom.

Bulk:
The mass or magnitude of something large.

Compliant/submissive fears:
Selfless fears such as: the fear of being killed, the fear he would harm my children, nowhere to go, embarrassed, and I would hurt him by leaving.

Contentment:
This is a state of happiness and satisfaction.

Courage:
Courage is the ability to do something that frightens you.

Counterfeit Emotions:
Counterfeit emotions also referred as masked emotions by the author, are untrue feelings that you display in front of others or to the other self in order to receive an expected response.

Denial:
The action of declaring something to be untrue when it is a fact. Denial can be a protective wall to protect you from acknowledging your real emotions and recognizing your hardships and pains.

Depression:
Feelings of severe despondency and dejection. A mental heal disorder characterized by persistently depressed mood or loss of interest in activities causing significant impairment in daily life.

Egocentric fears:
Selfish fears such as: the fear of being out of a relationship, not being sexually pleased, not having the financial help, and not having the honeymoon attention.

Emotions:
A natural instinctive state of mind deriving from one's circumstances, mood, or relationships with others.

Entrap:
To trick or deceive someone.

Fear:
This is an unpleasant emotion caused by the belief that someone or something is dangerous, likely to cause pain, and seen as a potential threat or harm.

Forgiveness:
This is an unpleasant emotion caused by the belief that someone or something is dangerous, likely to cause pain, and seen as a potential threat or harm.

Frustrate:
To prevent (a plan) from progressing, succeeding, or being fulfilled. To prevent (someone) from doing or achieving something.

Happiness:
Happiness is a state of well-being and gladness, as well as a gratifying or satisfying experience.

Hopeless Hinders:
Hindrances that aid in the disconnection in knowing our worth and achieving our purpose in life.

Instinctive needs:
The instinct need, to be loved, fed, protected, and nourished.

Masks:
A covering for all or part of the face, worn as a disguise, or to amuse or terrify other people.

Mental:
Relating to the mind.

Mixed:
Consisting of different qualities or elements.

Movable:
Capable of being moved

Pacify:
To quell the anger, agitation, or excitement. To bring a peace to a combative party when there is a threat

Pleasure:
Pleasure is an instinctive feeling of being happy, satisfied, and experiencing enjoyment and entertainment, contrasted with things done out of necessity.

Quicksand:
A loose and wet sand that yields easily to pressure and suck in anything resting on or falling into it.

Real Emotions:
Emotions/feelings that are instinctive and come naturally.

R.E.S.T.:
The acronym which stands for **R**ecognizing, **E**ncouraging, **S**trengthen/Strive and **T**eam build.

Sadness:

Sadness is usually associated with grief and discontent and is generally caused by sorrow or regret.

Sink:
Go down below the surface of something. Especially of a liquid to become submerged.

The Other Self:
Our altered ego or our inner inferiority.

The Priceless Rights:
Your individual inborn rights that no person shall ever violate.

The Priceless Rights Passage:
You have the right to say no, and through life set boundaries. You also have the right to be unharmed, and if anyone should violate your priceless rights; you also have the right to tell.

tres luces:
Translated as three lights and this is a meditation using three candles of different colors to go through the phases in achieving forgiveness.

Tres Luces Commitment:
We the nation shall find focus not to judge, hate, and destroy. We, my brothers and sisters shall find focus to be impartial, love, and create. Together, we will rebuild our hearts, spirits, homes, communities, states, and countries. *Tres Luces*.

Discomfort:

When there is an absence of comfort or ease and there is an experience of feeling of uneasiness, or mild pain.

Vampire Disease:

Another name the Author uses to describe depression.

Water:

A colorless, transparent, odorless, tasteless liquid that forms the seas lakes, rivers, and rain and is the basis of the fluids of living organisms.

ANSWER KEY

CHAPTER 1 YOU ARE PRICELESS (KNOWING YOUR WORTH)

a) Quicksand is loose and wet sand that yields easily to pressure and suck in anything resting on or falling into it.
b) Without a bottom.
c) Capable of being moved.
d) The mass or magnitude of something large.
e) Consisting of different qualities or elements.
f) A colorless, transparent, odorless, tasteless liquid that forms the seas lakes, rivers, and rain and is the basis of the fluids of living organisms.
g) Go down below the surface of something. Especially of a liquid to become submerged.
h) To trick or deceive someone.
i) To prevent (a plan) from progressing, succeeding, or being fulfilled. To prevent (someone) from doing or achieving something.
j) A natural instinctive state of mind deriving from one's circumstances, mood, or relationships with others.
k) Relating to the mind.

1) Your Answer
2) Your Answer
3) Your Answer
4) Psalm 139:13 & 14

1) [13]For thou has possessed my reins: thou hast covered me in my mother's womb. [14]I will praise thee; for I am fearfully and wonderfully made: marvelous are thy works; and that my soul knoweth right well.

5) When emotions such as fear, anger, happiness, or sadness prevent us from moving forward. See pages 13 & 14

6) Hinders our relationship with self
   a. Not knowing our worth
   b. Bitterness
   c. Fear
   d. Embarrassment
   e. Regret
   f. Secrecy
   g. Feeling emotionally deprived
   h. Robbed of justice from a wrong doing
   i. Lack of honest with our real emotion

7) Your Answer

8) Achieve happiness and peace
   a. Know your worth
   b. Know your likes
   c. Identify your hobbies by knowing your likes
   d. Define your purpose
   e. Embrace your worth.

9) True

10) False

11) True

12) True

13) False

14) False

15) True

CHAPTER 2 DEFINING AND WORKING THROUGH REAL EMOTIONS

1) Emotions/feelings that are instinctive and come naturally.

2) Counterfeit emotions also referred as masked emotions by the author, are untrue feelings that you display in front of others or to the other self in order to receive an expected response.

3) A covering for all or part of the face, worn as a disguise, or to amuse or terrify other people.

4) Anger is a strong feeling or annoyance, displeasure of hostility.

5) This is a state of happiness and satisfaction.

6) Sadness is usually associated with grief and discontent and is generally caused by sorrow or regret.

7) Happiness is a state of well-being and gladness, as well as gratifying or satisfying experience.

8) This is an unpleasant emotion caused by the belief that someone or something is dangerous, likely to cause pain, and seen as a potential threat or harm.

9) Courage is the ability to do something that frightens you.

10) Pleasure is an instinctive feeling of being happy, satisfied, and experiencing enjoyment and entertainment, contrasted with things done out of necessity.

11) When there is an absence of comfort or ease and there is an experience of feeling of uneasiness, or mild pain.

12) Our altered ego or inner inferiority.

13) The action of declaring something to be untrue when it is a fact.

14) To quell the anger, agitation, or excitement. To bring a peace to a combative party when there is a threat.

15) Real emotions are feelings that are instinctive and come natural and counterfeit or masked emotions are untrue feelings that you display in front of others or to the other self in order to receive an expected response or to protect yourself from showing your true feelings.

16) By embracing your real emotions, you are able to be honest with yourself in what is acceptable behavior towards you and able you to establish boundaries. Real emotions rid the ability for denial (the other self) to grow.

17) The lack of embracing our real emotions hinders our relationship with ourselves, God, and others that we are close to.

18) [a]satan   [b]Your Answer

19) Your Answer

CHAPTER 3 THE HOPELESS HINDERS

1) Aid the disconnection in knowing our worth and achieving our purpose in life.
2) Selfish fears such as: the fear of being out of a relationship, not being sexually pleased, not having the financial help, and not having the honeymoon attention.
3) Selfless fears such as: the fear of being killed, the fear he would harm my children, nowhere to go, embarrassed, and I would hurt him by leaving.
4) Feeling of sever despondency and dejection. A mental heal disorder characterized by persistently depressed mood or loss of interest in activities causing significant impairment in daily life.
5) Another name the Author uses to describe depression.
6) Translated from Spanish to English meaning three lights and this is a meditation using three candles of different colors to go through the phases in achieving forgiveness.
7) This is the acronym which stands for Recognizing, Encouraging, Strengthen/Strive and Team build.
8) This is an unpleasant emotion caused by the belief that someone or something is dangerous, likely to cause pain, and seen as a potential threat or harm.
9) We were born with the instinctive needs to be loved, fed, protected, and nourished.
10) When those instinctive needs are not met; real emotions are felt such as fear, discomfort, sadness, and anger.

11) "Do unto others as you would want them to do unto you."
12) Fear is not something that a person conjures up out of our heads to gain sympathy or attention.
13) Fear is:
   a. From a potential threat, and unwelcomed experience, a protector shield to ward off possible danger;
   b. May be a prison and substance for the emotional quick sand that submerges you and me into depression.
14) People may invent sicknesses or throw tantrums to avoid going to school because:
   a. Bullying
   b. Abuse
15) Intervention from bullying should occur at an early age.
16) Her spirit that has been shattered and broken.
17) She was never told how to overcome her grief, bullying, hardships, and pain. The Author also never was given a guide to aid in healing and knowing her worth. She is sharing her struggles and giving a guide that was not given to her.
18) The Author had to focus, learn, and realize to begin the process of healing and forgiveness:
   a. Focus on strengths and be honest with real emotions.
   b. Focus on what means the most to you in your life.

c. Realize you are not born to fear, anger, sadness, etc: fear, anger, sadness was born to you.

d. Learn that all through situations and some people impregnated you with those real emotions such as fear; it is your choice to give birth to it. If you birth it—you must discipline it and correct.

e. Realize that you have rights.

19) Some reasons people abuse or experience anxiety and depression are:

a. Fear

b. Unaddressed anger

c. Anger turned inward

d. Anger and fear are not addressed

20) The three rights declared by the Author are:

a. The right to say how you feel and if you have been offended.

b. The right to set boundaries and embrace your real emotions.

c. The right to talk to God about how you feel and know that there is no punishment for being honest.

21) The steps to dig your way out of depression are:

a. Embracing your real emotions will allow you to emerge from the emotional quicksand.

b. Addressing hopeless hinders and channeling forgiveness.

c. Incorporate R.E.S.T. into your daily living.

d. Remove the bulk perceptions.

22) The 7 beginning steps when coping with stress:
    a. Remind yourself that he/she is being used to dim your light.
    b. Think of a place that is calm and remind yourself of your blessings.
    c. Remind yourself that this person is going through their own storm and perhaps your light can be the beacon to guide them to spiritual change.
    d. Focus on your goals and what you want to achieve in life.
    e. Do not allow the enemy power over my spiritual wealth.
    f. Daily prayer and meditation.
        i.   The tres luces (three lights) meditation
        ii. Allow your strengths to be your coping skills.
23) The 4 Focuses
    a. Being impartial, loving, and creating.
    b. Sharing our testimonies, talents, and becoming the beacon of light for others that have gone through hardship.
    c. Mothers should focus on their children first.
    d. Fathers should focus on their children first.
24) True
25) True
26) True
27) True
28) True
29) True

30) False

31) True

32) True

33) True

34) False

35) False

CHAPTER 4 LOVING YOURSELF (THE PRICELESS RIGHTS)

1) Are your individual inborn rights that no person shall ever violate. The Priceless Rights Passage is, your right to say no, and through life set boundaries. You also have the right to be unharmed, and if anyone should violate your priceless right; you also have the right to tell.

2) We the nation shall find focus not to judge, hate, and destroy. We, my brothers and sisters shall find focus to be impartial, love, and create. Together, we will rebuild our hearts, spirits, homes, communities, states, and countries, *Tres Luces*.

3) You deserve happiness, peace, and a true relationship with you.
   a. Treat yourself to the movies, dinner, suite at the hotel, a good book.
   b. Converse with The LORD.
   c. Daily prayer and meditation

4) Two reason why it is time that you tell would what you have endured
   a. The power is taken away from the enemy
   b. It is time for everyone to take accountability for his/her actions.
5) The enemy will use others to try and dim our lights.
   a. When this happens, we must:
      i. Embrace your coping strategies.
      ii. Find focus on what is important not what is irrelevant and a deterrence for your God-given purpose.
6) True
7) False
8) False
9) True
10) True

Michelle Carter-Douglass

Behind These Closed Doors
A Work in Poetry

Behind these closed doors, there is a testimony of survival. Michelle Carter-Douglass finds perfection and, healing through imperfect trials and heartache.
Take an inspirational journey in poetry through this opened door. There is light after every dark storm.

105 pages in length.
Dimensions 6 x 0.27 x 9 inches.

Broken Mirrors and Mended Wounds
A Work in Poetry

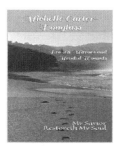

There is no place our Lord Thy God cannot reach. So broken were my soul and self-esteem. Through my journey, only God restored my soul and made me whole.

Tera Kirksey shares, "Broken Mirrors and Mended Wounds This collection of poems and reflections was so on point. They were so uplifting to me.

My favorite one was Revelation mended through being broken. I could truly relate to this one.

This author blessed my soul through her writing. I know she's at a point of healing! I'd love to read more from this author."

146 pages in length.
Dimensions 6 x 0.37 x 9 inches.

Poetic Intimacy
A Work in Poetry

Who says God-fearing women do not struggle with the desires of being loved and held? Newly divorced and devoted to raising her children, this author shares her journey through poetry from promiscuity to celibacy.

151 pages in length.
Dimensions 6 x 0.38 x 9 inches.

Behind Closed Doors Vol. 1

The WAR, the AFTERMATH, and the GLORY

A Work in Poetry

Behind every true story, there is a person. The smile I greeted people with was equivalent to an article of clothing I wore.

I was battered, broken, and enduring a great war behind closed doors. My relationship with my husband set me in flames. After this great war, my body lay broken upon the earth. Now, I am mended by The Grace of God and will share my testimony through opened doors.

166 pages in length.
Dimensions 6 x 0.42 x 9 inches.

In Darkness
The Poetic Hell
A Work in Poetry

It doesn't matter how many doors by man are closed. The depth of the dark shadows that the adversary throws your way will never define or devour you. In the darkness, our Heavenly Father shall provide the escape (Isaiah 60:2).

116 pages in length.
Dimensions 6 x 0.29 x 9 inches.

In Light

The Bride of Christ
A Work in Poetry

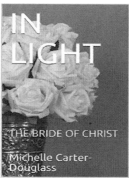

No single person on earth has a perfect life. Nonetheless, you and I have the perfect Christ. After all those painful storms, I learned true love. After the darkness, I am walking in Light.

47 pages in length.
Full-color interior.
Dimensions 6 x 0.12 x 9 inches.

Melodies
Poetic Truth Serum
A Work in Poetry

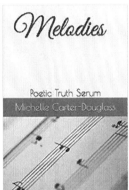

This world, our God created with words. Since the beginning of the creation of man and woman, you and I used words to build and words to tear down. Through melodies and songs, the world heals and continues to grow. Reader, my friend, grow with me through this book written in poetry, Melodies.

45 pages in length.
Dimensions 6 x 0.11 x 9 inches.

THE PROSPERITY PROJECT SERIES:
Restoring Your Inner Peace After Abuse

The brightest stars on earth have overcome many adversities in their lives. This book is dedicated to the inner healing of abuse victims and those who have encountered traumatic experiences. Focusing on the strength-based perspective, the reader will connect with their innate ability to overcome all obstacles.

Instructor's manual and the Individual student books are designed for facilitating workshops, bible studies, individual reading, and or groups.

Instructor's Manual:
143 pages in length.
Full-color.
Glossary.
Study guide and, activities.
Dimensions 8.5 x 0.34 x 11 inches.

Individual Book:
143 pages in length.
Glossary
Study guide and, activities.
Dimensions 6 x 0.36 x 9 inches.

Patrick M. Douglass

The Adventures of Gurgle Boy Vol 1.

With only a few minutes until they could exit Taconic State Parkway, the roads and traffic take a turn for the worse. Readers and Friends, the angel of death, was near. Sterile and John prayed silently to Almighty God.

Are they speared?

Everyone hopes for a perfect love story. Some people dream of taking an adventure. In a small town named Poughkeepsie, New York, a couple and six young adults will meet and change one another's lives forever.

126 pages in length.
Dimensions 6 x 0.32 x 9 inches.

Arlessa R. Douglass

In Our Storms We Have God

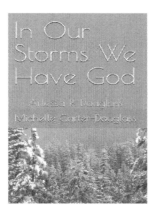

The following prayers are for the mind, spirit, body and, soul. Arlessa Douglass and her mother sit down and open their hearts and souls to the people of the world today. No matter what storm you are going through, you have God.

66 pages in length.
Dimensions 5 x 0.17 x 8 inches.

Christmas Morning

Each Christmas, the Douglass family will share their talents and a piece of their heart with you. An inspirational read for the Holidays. Amelia is in danger of losing her home and all hope this Christmas. Does Santa exist? Perhaps, the answer is prayer and kindness.

42 pages in length.
Full-color.
Dimensions 8.5 x 0.1 x 11 inches.

Brialan Douglass

My Purpose Ordained By God

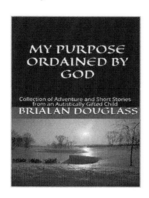

Brialan was a child broken down by bullying, child abuse and, being labeled. As a grown man, he stands firm that nothing and no one will ever tear down what God has built. Every single person born has a purpose. This heartfelt book will take you through an inspirational journey of adventure, mystery, and hope.

64 pages in length.
Dimensions 6 x 0.16 x 9 inches.

The Carter-Douglass and Douglass' Collaborative Works

In Our Storms We Have God II
Relationships, and Marriages Edition

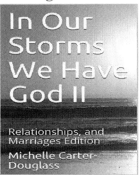

A mother, and her three special needs adult children embrace God through their happiness and struggles. In this book of prayers dedicated to The LORD ~ A mother, and her children share their experiences of how prayer brought them through their storms.

78 pages in length.
Dimensions 5 x 0.2 x 8 inches.

THE BEHIND CLOSED DOORS COLLECTION
In Darkness Presents: The Pandemic

eBook, Hardcover and, Paperback Covers pictured designed by Arlessa R. Douglass, Patrick M. Douglass and Brialan Douglass.

This book in poetry serves as a tool used to restore inner wealth and strength. In the middle of darkness bears the seed of light. At the core of this pandemic, we need to restore peace. There will always be natural disasters, diseases, wars, pain, and grief; nonetheless, do we have to create more turmoil? Or should we continue to find and heal God's sheep? Welcome once more behind the closed doors of the Carter and Douglass family through poetry.

eBook:
106 pages in length.
File size 3829 KB

Hardcover:
104 pages in length.
Dimensions 6 x 0.44 x 9 inches

Paperback:
Dimensions 6 x 0.24 x 9 inches

Raya, Isaac, Egypt, and Noah Presents:
The Resurrection Story

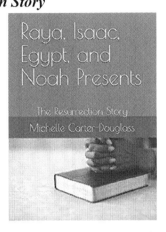

This book will take you on the journey from Creation through The Resurrection of our Lord and Savior, Jesus Christ. In this full-length color book, illustrated by authors Patrick M. Douglass, Brialan Douglass, and Arlessa R. Douglass, the authors answer questions, why do we dye boiled eggs, what's the significance of an Easter bunny, and more.

Hardcover:
162 pages in length.
Full-color
Dimensions 8.25 x 0.57 x 11 inches.

Paperback:
134 pages in length.
Full-color
Dimensions 8.5 x 0.32 x 11 inches.

THE PROSPERITY PROJECT SERIES:
Thinking Outside the Plantation

On the path to success, we find many adversities. What and to whom can be the stumbling blocks? Are we being spiritually punished for some things or, is something or someone trying to hinder us from receiving Almighty God's blessings?

Thinking Outside the Plantations is based on the Evidence-based Perspective. Evidence shows who and what is oppressing people today. The plantations of depression, suicide, domestic violence, and addictions will not define us. We have the power to become free. This book will guide you through breaking the chains, thus enabling you to step off those mental and philosophical plantations that impede your social growth.

This book is written by abuse survivors and designed for individual and group studies.

Instructor's manual and the Individual student books are designed for facilitating workshops, bible studies, individual reading, and or groups.

Instructor's Manual:
197 pages in length.
Full-color.
Glossary.
Study guide and activities.
Dimensions 8.5 x 0.47 x 11 inches.

Individual Book:
200 pages in length.
Glossary.
Study guide and activities.
Dimensions 7 x 0.46 x 10 inches.

Audio Works by Arlessa Reign

Available on CD Baby, iTunes, Spotify, and More

Thank You, Heavenly Father and our Lord, Jesus Christ!

Render by Arlessa Reign

Jilted by Arlessa Reign

https://store.cdbaby.com/cd/arlessareign

https://store.cdbaby.com/cd/arlessareign2

.

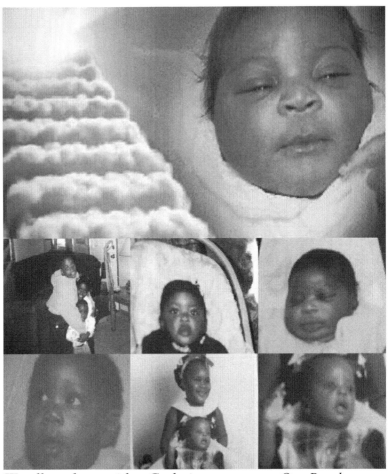

We all are born with a God-given purpose. Our Readers and Friends, do not give up and do not give in. Be a generation that thinks outside the plantation.

Author Social Media Contact Information

Author Patrick M. Douglass

https://www.facebook.com/patrick.douglass.14

https://www.facebook.com/Gurgleboy/

https://www.instagram.com/ravenblack1994/?hl=en

Arlessa R. Douglass
Arlessa Reign

https://www.facebook.com/profile.php?id=100025332611764

https://www.facebook.com/profile.php?id=100015620254715

https://www.instagram.com/arlessa_reign/?hl=en

Brialan Douglass

https://www.facebook.com/brialan.douglass.9

https://www.instagram.com/brialandouglass/?hl=en

Michelle Carter-Douglass

https://www.facebook.com/michelle.douglass.758

https://www.facebook.com/Mcarterdouglass

https://www.instagram.com/mcdbehindthesedoors/

I sincerely thank our Heavenly Father, Lord and Savior Jesus Christ, my family, friends, and each of you. I would not be here today if it were not for the trials, tribulations, and storms. Embrace the hard times, for it will make you a stronger person.

Michelle Carter-Douglass

Made in the USA
Middletown, DE
09 June 2022

66660596R00111